Magic

HANDBOOK

JOE FULLMAN

QEB Publishing

Copyright © QEB Publishing, Inc. 2008

Published in the United States by
QEB Publishing, Inc.
3 Wrigley, Suite A
Irvine, CA 92618

www.qed-publishing.co.uk

Library of Congress Control Number: 2008010183

ISBN 978 1 60992 347 1

Printed in China

Author Joe Fullman
Editor Amanda Askew
Designer Jackie Palmer
Illustrator Mark Turner for Beehive Illustrations

Picture credits
Corbis Bettmann 6, Hulton-Deutsch Collection 18
Getty Images Hulton Archive/ Stringer 11, Hulton Archive/
Stringer 13, Ethan Miller/Staff 24, Paul Drinkwater/Contributor/
WireImage 28
Topham 32

Contents

Rope and coin magic

A rope is cut in half and is then complete again, a coin appears to vanish beneath a glass, a ball magically rises into the air—what amazing magic! Using everyday items such as coins and pieces of string, you will learn how to do magic tricks guaranteed to astound your friends and family.

③ Difficulty rating

The tricks get harder throughout the book, so each trick has been given a rating. One is the easiest and seven is the hardest. The most difficult tricks will take a bit of practise to get right, but the results will be worth it!

① Preparation

Sometimes you will need to prepare something beforehand to make a trick work.

② New Skills Alert

As you practise the tricks, you will learn several new skills, such as "tying a false knot." You will also learn "sleight of hand" techniques, so you can do the tricks without your audience seeing what you are doing.

Playing to the crowd

The point of any good magic trick is to amaze and entertain your audience. While the trick will take care of the amazing part, it is up to you to do the entertaining. Telling jokes and stories while you perform your tricks will make your act even more enjoyable.

Two into one

In this trick, you will use some simple sleight hand to stun your audience—by making t pieces of rope become one!

NEW SKILLS ALERT

② Sleight of hand

One of the most important skills a magician can learn, sleight of hand means to move something without your audience seeing what you are doing. When you hide something in your hand or pretend to put something in your pocket, you are performing sleight of hand.

① Prep

⑥

Top Tip!

Make sure you don't tie the short rope around the long rope too tightly, or you will not be able to slide it off.

20

(4) Props needed...

The props you will need for each trick.

- Bag
- Coins
- Double-sided scotch tape
- Glass
- Glue
- Handkerchief
- Rope or string

- Light, plastic ball
- Paper
- Pencil
- Scissors
- Scotch tape
- Table
- Thread

(5) Stages and illustrations

Step-by-step instructions, as well as illustrations, will guide you through each trick.

1 Take out your prepared rope and tell your audience that it is a loop made from two short pieces of rope tied together. Only you will know that it is actually one long piece of rope and one short piece of rope.

2 Tell your audience that the ropes were tied together using two types of knot. The first is just a normal knot. As you say this, undo the knot holding the ends of the long piece of rope together.

Bringing back magic

Magic has not always been popular. After a boom in the late 19th and early 20th centuries, magic shows began to attract fewer people following the invention of film and television. Magic came to be seen as boring and old fashioned.

▶ Doug Henning was a Canadian magician who helped make magic popular again in the 1970s with his energetic performance and colorful clothes.

21

(6) Top Tip!

Hints and tips help you to perform the tricks better!

(7) Famous magicians and illusions

Find out who are the most exciting and skillful magicians, and what amazing feats they have performed.

The magic hole

This simple challenge is a good way to get started. Hand your volunteer the piece of paper and the larger coin. Ask them to try to pass the larger coin through the hole without tearing the paper. When they give up, show them how it is done.

Props needed...

* Piece of paper about 5 inches by 5 inches
* Scissors
* Two coins of slightly different sizes, such as a dime and a nickel

The most famous magician in the world

Born in Hungary in 1874, Eric Weiss moved to the U.S. with his family when he was just four years old. There he would grow up to become the best-known magician in the world, performing under the stage name, Harry Houdini. He was particularly famed for his feats of escapology—he escaped from many devices, including handcuffs, chains, straitjackets, and water-filled tanks.

▶ Harry Houdini escapes from a straitjacket while suspended above a crowd of people in New York City.

Preparation

• Take the smaller coin, place it in the center of your piece of paper and draw a circle around it.

• Using scissors, carefully cut out around the circle to make a hole.

6

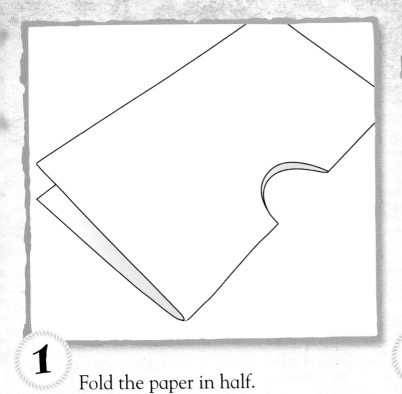

1 Fold the paper in half.

2 Drop the larger coin into the pouch formed by the paper.

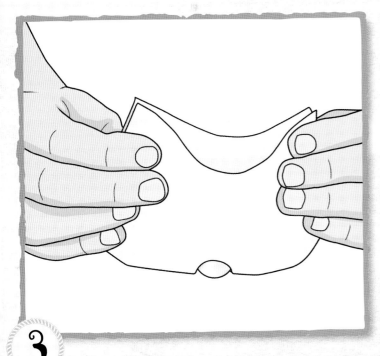

3 Push the ends of the paper together. This will increase the size of the hole.

4 Keep pushing and the hole will eventually be big enough for the larger coin to fall through, without tearing the paper. Magic!

Cross-armed knot

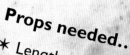

★ ★

This challenge is a great one to try at parties. Take the length of rope and hand it to a volunteer from your audience. Ask them to grip one end of the rope with one hand and the other end with the other hand. Now challenge them to tie a knot in the rope without releasing their grip. When they give up, show them how it is done.

Props needed...
* Length of rope or string, about 2 feet long
* Table

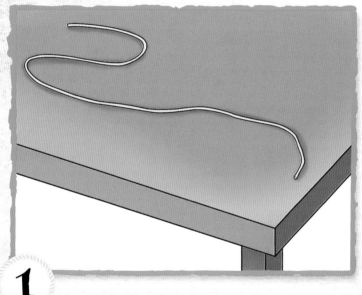

1 Lay the rope in front of you on a flat surface, such as a table.

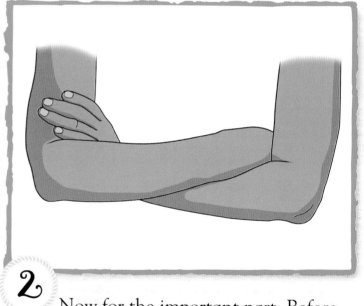

2 Now for the important part. Before you pick up the rope, fold your arms, so that one hand is resting on top, and one hand is tucked underneath.

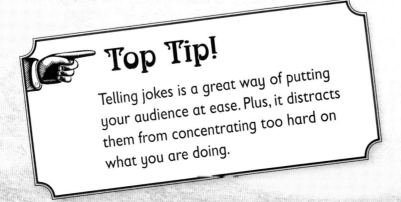

Top Tip!

Telling jokes is a great way of putting your audience at ease. Plus, it distracts them from concentrating too hard on what you are doing.

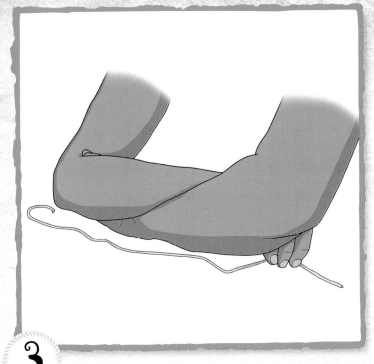

3 With your arms folded, lean forward and pick up one end of the rope using the hand that is tucked underneath.

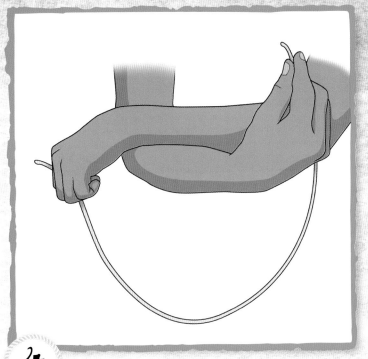

4 Grab the other end of the rope with the hand that is resting on top.

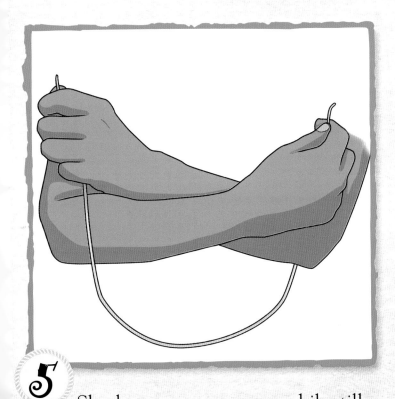

5 Slowly uncross your arms, while still holding on to the rope.

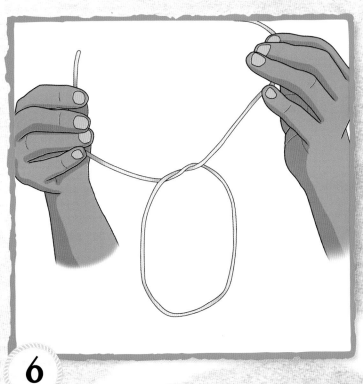

6 As your hands pass by each other, a loop will form in the center of the rope. Keep pulling and you will have a knot —without ever letting go of the rope.

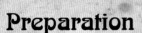

The coin bag

★ ★

For this trick, you need to do a little acting to convince your audience that you are a magical master!

Props needed...
* Bag
* Coins, each with a different date
* Table

Preparation

Before facing your audience, put the coins into your bag and then put the bag into the refrigerator for a few minutes. This will make the coins slightly colder than room temperature—which is important for the trick to work. Don't make them so cold that your audience will notice.

1 Place the bag of coins on the table in front of you. Ask a volunteer from the audience to approach the table.

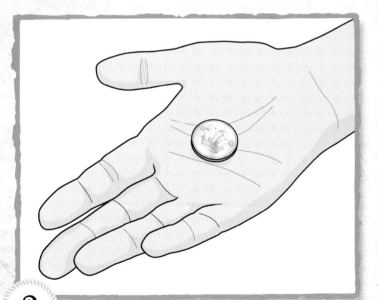

2 Now turn your back and ask them to pick a coin from the bag. Tell them to look at the date on the coin and remember it.

3 Tell them to close their fingers around the coin and to think of the coin's date. Turn back and tell your volunteer that you are going to try to read their mind. Stare at their face, as if you are trying to read their thoughts.

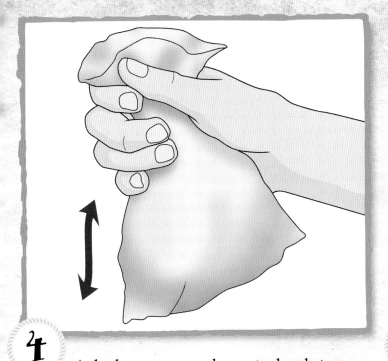

4 Ask them to put the coin back into the bag and to give it a thorough shake to mix all the coins up.

5 The secret of this trick is body temperature. By holding the coin in their hand, your volunteer will have made it much warmer than all the other coins. All you have to do now is reach inside the bag and pick out the coin that feels warmer than the rest.

Magic in the family

In the 19th century, the British magician John Maskelyne performed a well-known magic act with his partner George Cooke at a specially built London theater, the Egyptian Hall. They were the first people to perform the illusion of levitation. Maskelyne's son Nevil was also a magician, as was his son, Jasper. In World War II, Jasper used his talents to trick the enemy by creating fake tanks and planes.

▶ A ticket for Maskelyne and Cooke's famous magic act, which they used to perform twice a day at the Egyptian Hall Theater.

6 Pull out their coin and tell them the date. Now ask your volunteer to tip all the other coins onto the table and to check them, so they can see that all the coins have different dates.

The knot is gone!

For this trick, you will need to learn how to tie a "false knot"—a knot that looks like a real knot, but will untie itself when you pull on both ends of the rope. You will need to practise tying the knot before performing the trick, so you can do it quickly and easily.

Props needed...

* Handkerchief
* Length of rope or string

NEW SKILLS ALERT

How to tie a false knot

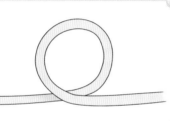

1 Take your rope and twist it into a circle.

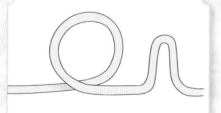

2 Now, form a loop in the rope, just to the right of the circle.

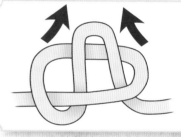

3 Take the loop and tuck it up into the circle.

4 Take hold of the top of the loop with the finger and thumb of your right hand. Grip the rope to the right of the loop with your other three fingers. Now, use your left hand to pull the left end of the rope, so that the circle wraps tightly around the loop.

1

Take out a length of rope and a handkerchief and show them to your audience. Ask a volunteer to examine them closely, so they can see there is nothing unusual about them.

2

Take the rope back and tie a false knot in it, in view of the audience.

4

Pull gently on the rope while the knot is under the handkerchief.

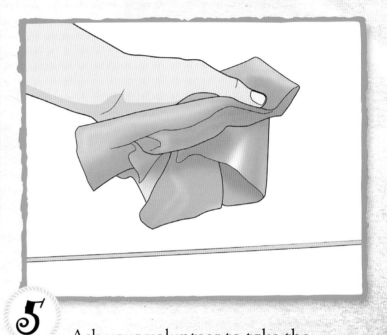

3

Holding the rope by its ends, ask your volunteer to place the handkerchief over the knot.

5

Ask your volunteer to take the handkerchief off the rope. The knot has magically disappeared.

Bringing back magic

Magic has not always been popular. After a boom in the late 19th and early 20th centuries, magic shows began to attract fewer people following the invention of film and television. Magic came to be seen as boring and old fashioned.

▶ Doug Henning was a Canadian magician who helped make magic popular again in the 1970s with his energetic performance and colorful clothes.

The vanishing coin

Amaze your audience by magically making a coin disappear and reappear.

Props needed...
* Coin
* Glass
* Glue
* Handkerchief
* Pencil
* Scissors
* Two large sheets of white paper

Preparation

1 Take one of the large pieces of paper and lay it down flat.

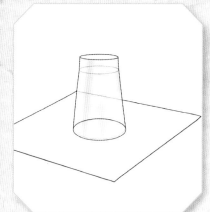

2 Place your glass on top of it with the mouth facing downward.

3 Using a pencil, trace around the outline of the glass.

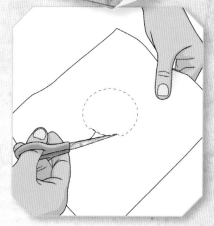

4 Carefully cut along the pencil line, so that you are left with a circle of paper.

6 Before your audience is in position, place the coin, the prepared glass, and the handkerchief on top of the other piece of paper.

5 Line the rim of your glass with glue and stick the paper circle on top. Once the glue is dry, cut off any extra paper.

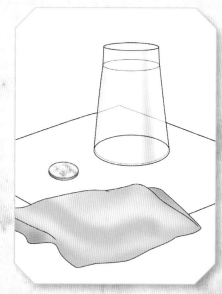

1 Announce to your audience that you are going to make the coin disappear. Now pick up the handkerchief and place it over the glass.

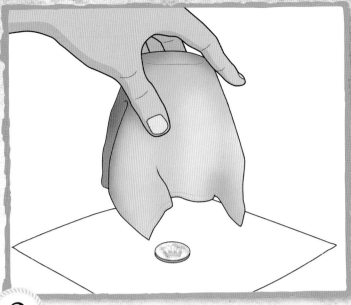

2 Place the handkerchief and glass over the coin that is sitting on the paper.

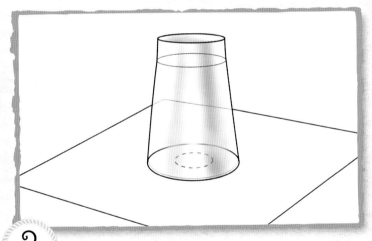

3 Take away the handkerchief to show that the coin has vanished, or so it will seem to your audience. Of course, you know that the coin is just hidden by the paper stuck to the glass, which is the same color as the paper below.

4 Put the handkerchief back over the glass.

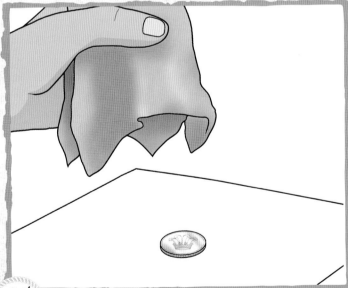

5 Lift up the handkerchief and the glass to reveal that the coin has now magically reappeared.

 **Top Tip!**
Use a thin coin, so that its shape does not show through the paper.

One-handed knot

In this trick, you will show your audience a length of rope, take it in one hand, make a few quick movements and magically you will have tied a knot, using just one hand. You need to practise, but the amazed looks on your friends' faces will make the effort worth it!

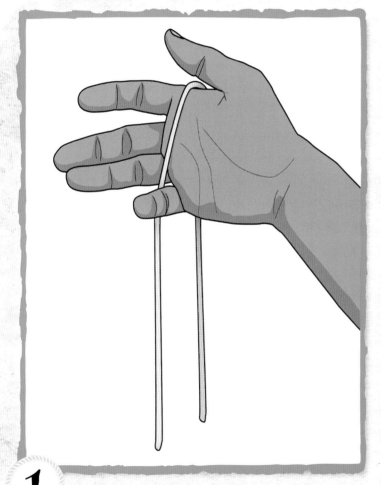

1 Drape the rope over your hand so that one end is hanging between your third finger and your little finger.

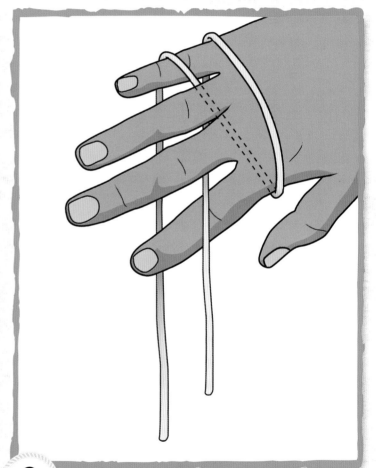

2 Now turn your hand the other way up, and then catch the other end between your first and second fingers.

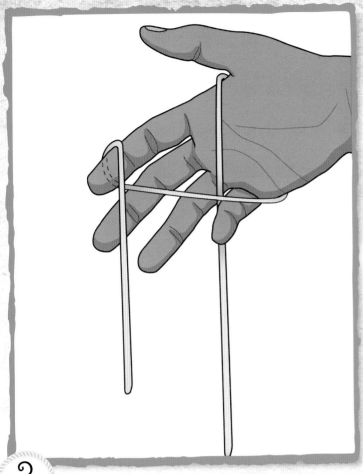

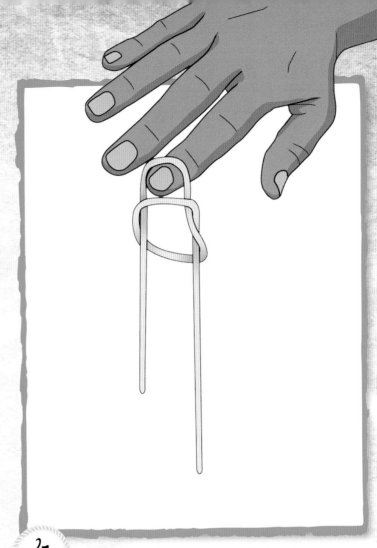

3 Turn your hand again, so your thumb is once again facing up.

4 Keeping hold of the rope between your first and second finger, point your fingers down, and let the rest of the rope slide off your hand.

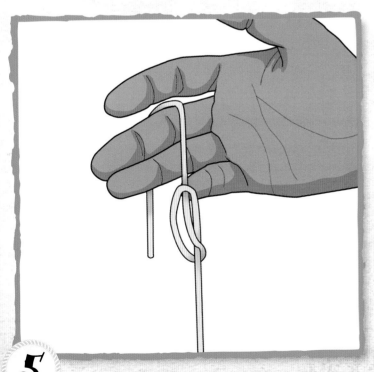

☞ **Top Tip!**

Once you have mastered the technique, you can try it with the other hand. See if you can tie two knots in a long piece of rope at the same time.

5 As the rope slides off, it will tie itself into a knot.

The sticky nail

Use a small piece of scotch tape to make it look like a coin has disappeared.

On the high wire

He may not have been a magician, but "The Great Blondin" performed many amazing feats during his career. His speciality was tightrope walking. In his act, he would walk on stilts, turn somersaults, and even carry someone on his back—all while balanced on a high rope. He became world famous in 1859 when he crossed Niagara Falls, on a tightrope 1,100 feet in length.

▼ *Charles Blondin, the French acrobat, performs a tightrope walk high above Niagara Falls.*

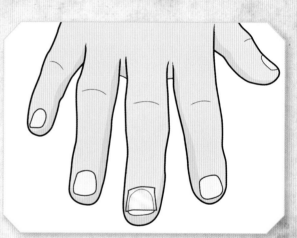

Preparation

• Take a small piece of double-sided scotch tape and place it on the nail that is nearest to the coin.

• Put the coin in your pocket.

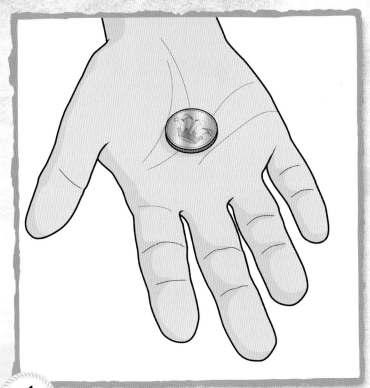

1 Show your empty hands to the audience. Keep your nails turned toward you, so that the audience cannot see the piece of tape. Take the coin from your pocket and place it in the palm of your hand.

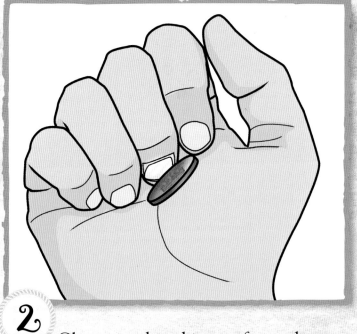

2 Close your hand into a fist and press the nail with the scotch tape onto the coin.

3 Wave your other hand over your closed fingers in a "magical" way to block your audience's view.

5 To get rid of the coin, put your hand in your pocket and let the coin fall off your finger.

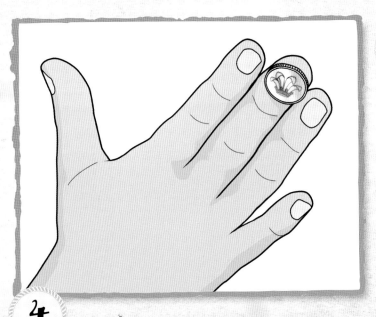

4 Now, quickly open your hand to show that the coin has disappeared. Only you will know that it is stuck to your nail.

Top Tip!

The lighter in weight the coin is, the easier this trick will be.

Two into one

In this trick, you will use some simple sleight of hand to stun your audience—by making two pieces of rope become one!

Props needed...
* Two lengths of rope—one long, one short

NEW SKILLS ALERT

Sleight of hand

One of the most important skills a magician can learn, sleight of hand means to move something without your audience seeing what you are doing. When you hide something in your hand or pretend to put something in your pocket, you are performing sleight of hand.

Preparation

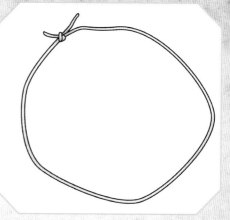

• Take the long piece of rope and tie the ends together into a knot, forming a loop.

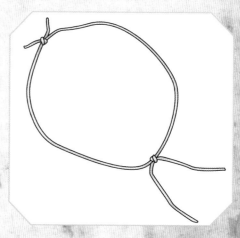

• Now take the smaller piece of rope and tie it around the longer piece on the opposite side to the first knot. This will make it look like the loop is made of two short pieces of rope tied together.

Top Tip!

Make sure you don't tie the short rope around the long rope too tightly, or you will not be able to slide it off.

20

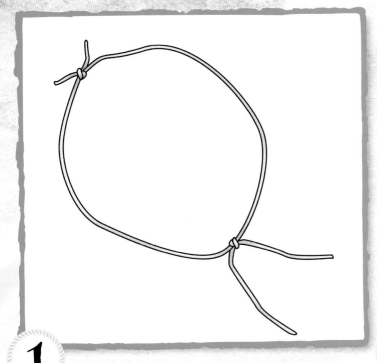

1 Take out your prepared rope and tell your audience that it is a loop made from two short pieces of rope tied together. Only you will know that it is actually one long piece of rope and one short piece of rope.

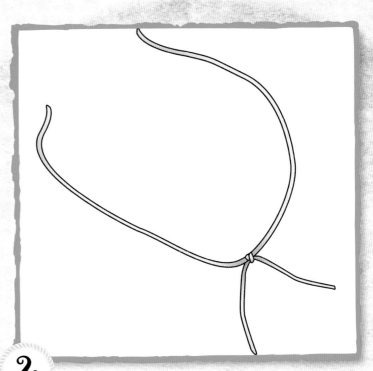

2 Tell your audience that the ropes were tied together using two types of knot. The first is just a normal knot. As you say this, undo the knot holding the ends of the long piece of rope together.

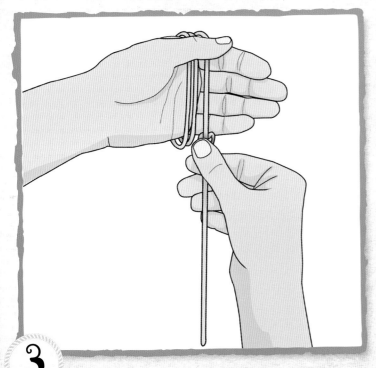

3 Start winding the rope around your hand. As you wind, slide the knot made from the short piece of rope off into your winding hand.

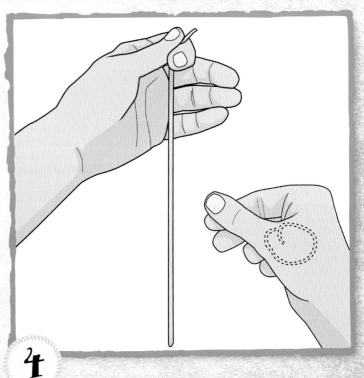

4 Keeping the short piece of rope hidden in one hand, show your audience that the two "short pieces" of rope have now become one!

Magic paper

Props needed...
* Coin
* Piece of paper, 5 inches by 5 inches

You take out a coin and place it in the center of a small square of paper. You fold the paper around the coin, say a few magic words, and then tear the paper into pieces. The coin has vanished. But how?

1 Place your coin in the center of the paper.

2 Now fold the bottom edge up until it is about a quarter of an inch from the top.

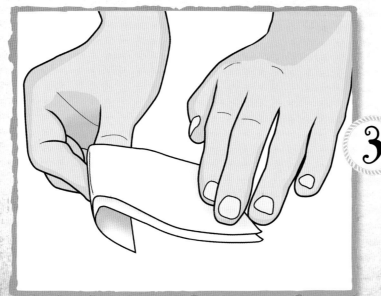

3 Fold the right-hand side of the paper behind the coin.

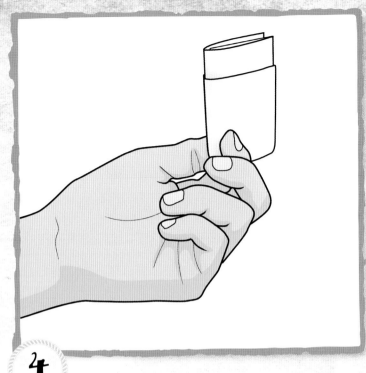

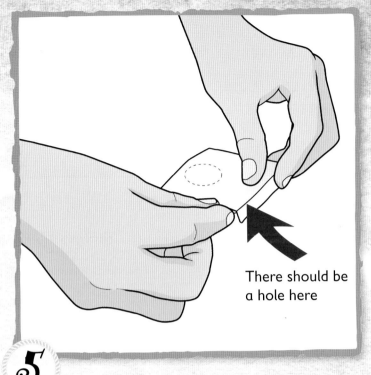

There should be
a hole here

4 Fold the left-hand side of the paper behind the coin.

5 Fold the top flap of paper behind the coin. To the audience this will look like the coin has been completely sealed in. In fact, if you have folded the paper correctly, there will be hole at the top.

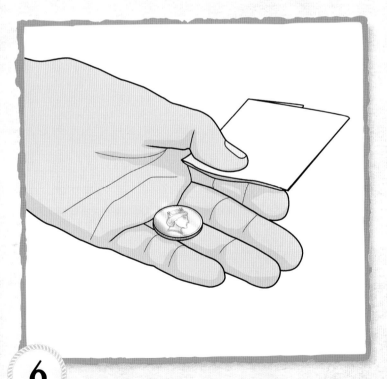

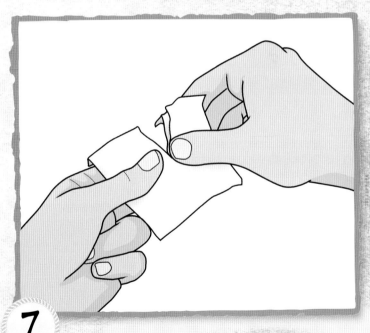

6 You will now need to perform sleight of hand. Turn the paper upside down and, without letting the audience see, allow the coin to fall into your hand.

7 Keeping the coin hidden in your hand, tear the paper in half and then in half again. The coin has vanished.

Balancing the ball

In this trick, it will look like you are rolling a ball along a piece of rope. In fact you are going to get some invisible assistance.

Props needed...
* Length of rope
* Length of thin thread, the same length as the rope
* Light, plastic ball
* Table

Preparation

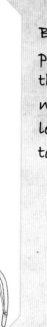

Before performing this trick, you need to attach a length of thread to the rope.

When the magic doesn't work

Even professional magicians sometimes get it wrong. In 2007, in Las Vegas, magician Nathan Burton attempted to spend 24 hours trapped inside an ice sculpture. Unfortunately the day on which he chose to perform his trick was so hot that the ice quickly began to melt and the attempt was called off after just a few hours, leaving Burton feeling embarrassed—and wet!

▼ Burton peers out from his rapidly melting ice prison.

Top Tip!

Keep a distance from your audience when you perform this trick, so they cannot spot the thread. Do not let anyone inspect the rope after the trick.

1 Lay the length of rope on a table and place a plastic ball in front of it.

2 When you lift the ball, you are going to pick it up between the rope and the thread—it will look to the audience as if you are just using the rope.

3 Impossible as it seems, start rolling the ball backward and forward along the rope. Make sure your audience does not look too closely.

4 Watch how amazed your audience is as you throw the ball in the air and catch it again on the rope.

The handshake

Watch your friends gasp in amazement as a coin appears to travel right through your hand.

Props needed...
* Coin

1 Place a coin in the palm of your hand and close your fingers around it, making a fist.

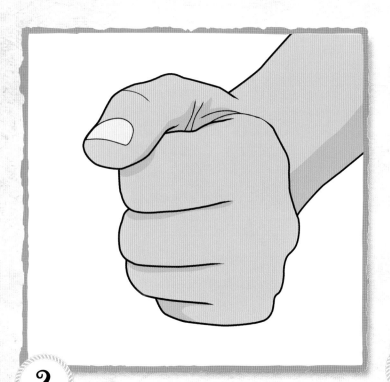

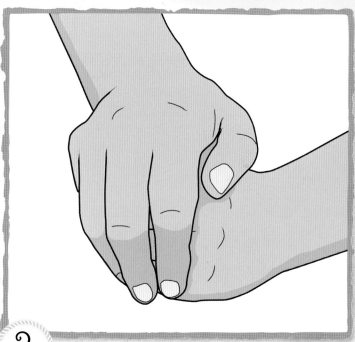

2 Turn your fist over, so that your thumb is facing upward.

3 Take your other hand and place it over your fist, so that the fingers are at the front, facing your audience.

Top Tip!
The quicker you can perform this trick, the more convincing it will seem.

4 Say the magic word "abracadabra" and start shaking your hands up and down.

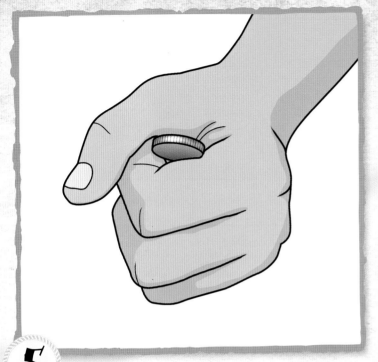

5 Make sure the top hand is pressing down tightly on the one below, but loosen the grip of the hand holding the coin. As you shake your hands, the coin will pop up between the thumb and first finger of your fist.

6 Keep shaking and use the top hand to slide the coin on top of your other hand, out of sight of your audience. The shaking will make it difficult for the audience to see exactly what you are doing.

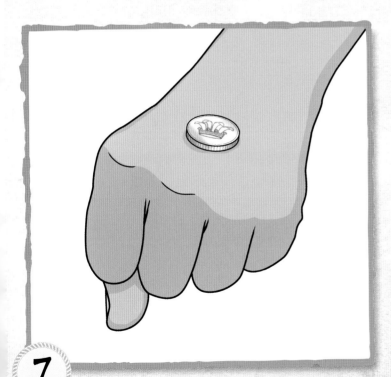

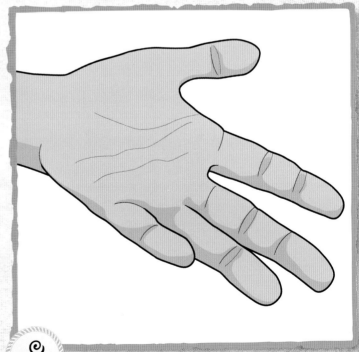

7 Take your top hand away to show that the coin is now sitting on top of the lower hand.

8 Pick up the coin and turn over your hand, showing the audience that the coin is not in your hand—it has traveled all the way through!

The magic rope

Holding a long length of rope in your hand, you cut the rope in half, making two short ropes. You say the magic word, "abracadabra," and release your hand to reveal that the rope has been magically restored to its full length! Cue audience amazement. You will need to practise sleight of hand to get this trick to work.

Preparation

• Before you start this trick, take the short length of rope and curl it into a narrow loop.

• Stick the ends together with scotch tape, so it holds its shape. Then hide the loop in your hand.

• Put the long piece of rope in your jacket pocket.

The capital of magic

More magic shows are performed every year in the city of Las Vegas than anywhere else in the world. Many of the city's casinos have large theaters where lavish magic shows—complete with explosions, light shows and performing animals—are put on. Several of the world's most popular magicians have performed here, including David Copperfield, Lance Burton, and Criss Angel.

◄ Lance Burton levitates actress Pamela Anderson during his Las Vegas magic show.

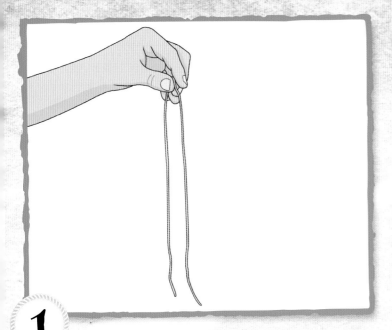

1 Keep the hand holding the short length of rope hanging casually by your side. Take the long length of rope out of your pocket. Hold it by one end to show the audience that it is one long piece of rope. Then, take hold of it in the middle, so that it hangs as two strands.

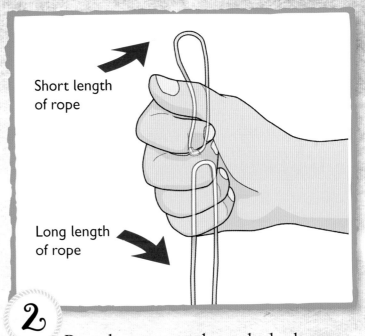

Short length of rope

Long length of rope

2 Pass the rope up through the bottom of your other hand. Feed it about half way up, and leave it there. Now transfer your grip to the small loop already in your hand. Pull the end of this small loop out of the top of your hand.

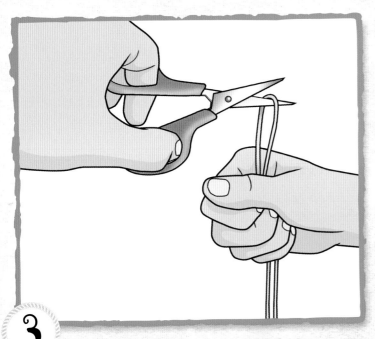

3 Ask a volunteer to carefully cut through the small loop sticking out the top of your hand. The audience will think they have cut the long rope.

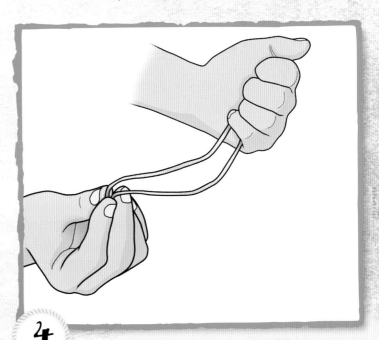

4 Wave your free hand over the rope. This will obscure your audience's view. Now tuck the cut ends of the small loop back into your hand and pull out the long length of rope, showing that it is whole again.

The sticky hand

This clever piece of sleight of hand will take a bit of practise to get right.

Props needed...
* Coin
* Glue

Preparation

Before facing your audience, put a small amount of glue onto the back of your hand.

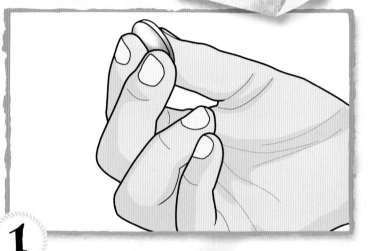

1 Hold the coin between your thumb and first two fingers of your non-sticky hand, and show it to your audience.

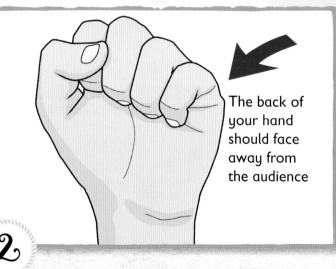

The back of your hand should face away from the audience

2 Make a fist with your sticky hand. Hold the fist up, so the back of your hand is facing you.

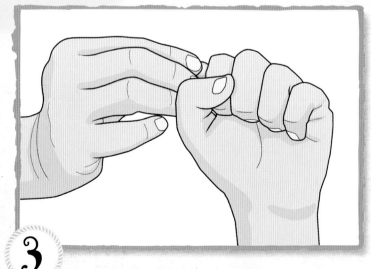

3 Tell the audience that you are going to put the coin inside your fist. Using your thumb and the first two fingers of your non-sticky hand, place the coin at the opening of your fist.

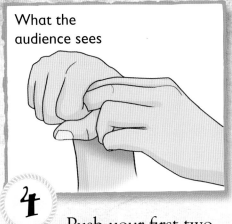

What the audience sees

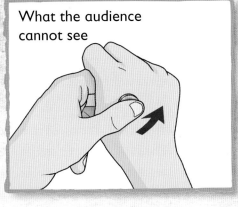

What the audience cannot see

4 Push your first two fingers into your fist as if you were pushing the coin inside. These fingers will cover the audience's view of your thumb.

At the same time, use your thumb to push the coin, out of sight of your audience, onto the back of your hand where it will stick to the glue.

5 With the coin in position, pull your fingers out and wave them over the closed fist. Say the magic word, "abracadabra."

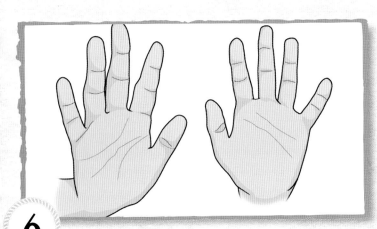

6 Open you hands, palm up to the audience, to show that the coin has vanished.

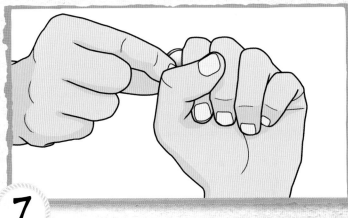

7 Now announce that you are going to bring the coin back. Close your hand back into a fist, and place the two fingers of your non-sticky hand inside.

8 Slowly remove your fingers. As you do, use your thumb to slide the coin from the back of your hand into your fist.

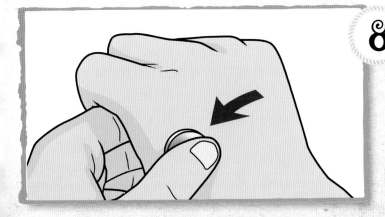

9 Once the coin is inside your fist take your other hand away, open your palm and reveal the coin.

The greatest illusion

The Indian rope trick is one of the world's most famous illusions—or is it the world's greatest fake?

In the trick, a magician throws a rope up into the air. However, instead of falling back to the ground, the rope stands stiff and upright. The magician's assistant then climbs the rope and, when he reaches the top, disappears, at which point the rope collapses. After a few moments, the assistant then reappears back on the ground.

Supposedly the trick has been performed in India for centuries. However, some people doubt whether it really exists, believing stories about the trick to be "tall tales." Certainly there is no film or television footage of anyone having performed the trick. It has even been claimed that the trick was invented by a U.S. newspaper reporter in 1890 to get publicity for his paper.

The Magic Circle, a society of British magicians, became so convinced that the trick was a fake that they offered a large cash prize to anyone who could recreate it at their headquarters in London, England. No one ever claimed the prize.

▲ A magician's assistant begins to climb the rope, but will they disappear?